EXIT
STRATEGY

The Employee Stock Ownership Plan Can Sustain and Secure the Company's Future Without You

EXIT
STRATEGY

The Employee Stock Ownership Plan Can Sustain and Secure the Company's Future Without You

This process shall expose strengths and weaknesses. A proper exit strategy will shore up the future.

ANTHONY (TONY) THOMPSON
MISSION POSSIBLE PRESS, USA
Creating Legacies through Absolute Good Works
Professional Development Series

The Mission is Possible.

Sharing love and wisdom for the young and "the young at heart," expanding minds, restoring kindness through good thoughts, feelings, and attitudes is our intent. May you thrive and be good in all you are and all you do…

Be Cause U.R. Absolute Good!

Exit Strategy, *The Employee Stock Ownership Plan Can Sustain and Secure the Company's Future Without You*

Published by
MISSION POSSIBLE PRESS
A Division of Absolute Good
P.O. Box 8039, St. Louis, MO 63156
orders@absolutegood.com

ISBN 978-0-9861818-0-1

DEDICATION

To my parents,
Jack & Betty Thompson and my wife Kim.
Thanks to each of you, this journey has been possible.

৩৽৹

CONTENTS

FOREWORD

Like most entrepreneurs, Tony Thompson spent a significant part of his life focused on building a successful business. He accomplished this through a combination of education, hard work, dedication, team building and collaboration. As Tony looked to develop a plan to exit the business he relied on those same attributes to help him choose the best exit option.

In his book Exit Strategy, Tony Thompson explores the process that he went through and the path he ultimately selected. Tony spent a considerable amount of time investigating his exit options in order to find the best solution based on his interests. There is no one size fits all strategy to exiting a business, thus it is important for the business owner to understand all of their alternatives both from a financial and psychological context.

For most entrepreneurs, exiting the business extends far beyond a simple monetary event. Legacy, loyalty, and a desire to shepherd a smooth transition were all elements of critical importance to Tony. Ultimately, Tony utilized an ESOP strategy that aligned with his corporate vision. Committed and diligent, Tony was able to proceed with confidence knowing that the ESOP was the right choice based on his desired legacy. Whether or not this same choice is appropriate for others, the process of personal reflection and education that are outlined in this book are critical to a successful business transition.

David M. Diehl, CFA,
Chief Operating Officer,
Prairie Capital Advisors, Inc.

WHAT'S NEXT?

———●———

What are you going to do with all of your hard work?

As the passionate builder of this business, there were things I had to seriously consider as I was making the choice to convert ownership.

There's a point when we aren't sure what to do with what we've built. Depending on the industry, the question becomes, "Who will I sell it to?" There may not be many buyers, especially for small businesses.

Even if you are a new business owner, start out with an end in mind. It's never too early to know where and how you want to finish. So, even if you have one or two paralegals or attorneys, it would be wise to offer them a piece of the action. If you say, "At the right time, I would like to offer the company to you," you are grooming them for a mutually beneficial future.

There are many mature business owners, my age or older, whose kids have no interest in business. Some of us are tired. We lack the energy to keep pushing, and some have failing health. We keep going to the office because we don't know what else to do. If we don't keep going, the business will fall apart.

The Employee Stock Ownership Plan Can Sustain and Secure the Company's Future Without You – with an Exit Strategy.

A New Direction

———👤———

Looking at the results of twenty plus years of building my business makes me pleased with our progress, humble and a bit apprehensive at the same time. I have never really regretted most of the decisions I made as CEO of my company yet, exiting isn't easy. The hunger, the passion, the relentless focus, hard work, sleepless nights and, at times, painful choices were cornerstones of my daily life. In the beginning it was the need for working capital driving me to new levels. Then it was consumer demand forcing us to grow and expand. As times, and technology changed, experience taught me to focus less on creating more revenue, and to focus more on profitability.

On July 23, 1991 I incorporated the Kwame Building Group as a Program/Construction Management firm located in St. Louis, Missouri. Our primary business is to act as an agent for owners who are embarking on construction related projects. We work on projects ranging from healthcare, transportation, educational facilities to wastewater treatment facilities nationwide. We are responsible for managing projects from conceptualization to construction completion. When I started this endeavor, there wasn't much competition. My business fulfilled a need; insuring projects would be completed on time, under budget and with the highest quality. For over 20 years I've been able to do just that.

Continually evolving, mostly due to external factors, I found myself looking around and back, realizing that just as my children, bank account, and staff had grown, so had my desire to pursue other interests. Wanting the time and space to do more, in different, meaningful ways, I enjoy mentoring small business owners and sharing the experience and knowledge I've gained in 23 years of business. I was ready for new things. My people, many loyal, dedicated people who had been with me for the lifespan of the company deserved more. I wasn't exactly tired, yet I wasn't as hungry. Knowing my time "in charge" needed to end brought mixed feelings of excitement and tension with thoughts of practicality and reality.

I did get an offer for my company a few years back. That was the first time I started thinking about acquisitions. I could have sold it to them. They would have made money and then fired all of my people. Selling the company outright, to the right buyer could offer immediate reward however, once the company is sold, all bets are off, you can't protect the employees and you can't control how or what the new owners do.

Still fairly young, I wasn't ready to retire. What would I do with the company? If I called it quits, I knew I couldn't see those years of hard work, evaporate into nothingness. Our company, our legacy served as a compass for friends, families, colleagues and clients who depended on us for all sorts of things, the least of which were salaries, benefits, revenues, referrals and services. I had to find a way to create mutual benefit while being true to my life, my wife and our collective future.

As I explored options, the top three choices were to sell the company outright, shut it down, or create an Exit Strategy which would preserve the organization while also generating retirement funds for each of us, for the long haul.

I chose the Employee Stock Ownership Plan (ESOP) route. An ESOP is a "qualified employee retirement plan" designed to invest primarily in stock of the sponsoring company.

Priorities May Be Different

My spirit of entrepreneurialism is different than others. When I was the sole owner of the company I could make major decisions about giving, spending and long-term financial commitments autonomously. Once the ESOP is in place, it's not that simple. Therefore, it's necessary to clarify what will be continued or not based on practicalities and realities versus the owner's original/singular vision or passion. In other words, what was important to you may not be important to the employee owners. You must think about this carefully and decide what priorities will be – and then seek buy-in within the new structure as to whether the programs will continue.

Ownership Conversion

Now, employees are shared owners in the company, where as I was the sole owner prior to the ESOP transaction. Once the transaction occurred, I basically gave them half of my company, which they did not have to pay for. The profits from the company paid for it. So what I did, I gave up future profits to pay off the loan that the company took out to buy me out in order that the employees can now own that half.

I wanted to share with the people that helped get me here. They helped me build the company so they needed to reap some of the benefits beyond just a paycheck. The reward is in retirement, because most of the people who work in this company hadn't been participating in the 401K offered before I did the ESOP. Previously, I set up a 401K plan and the company even matched the plan. Can you believe that less than half of the employees participated? That was money that they would have to invest for their future, for retirement. They wouldn't even do it even when we matched it.

Employees still get their checks every two weeks, so that didn't change. Yet, by creating the ESOP new structure, investing in retirement, they have to continue to work, but the difference is, the more profitable the company becomes, the more the company is worth. As they increase the value of the company, their share allocations increase when they retire.

The other side of this coin is, it's like a 401K in the sense that, they don't necessarily have to wait until full retirement. Their allocations are distributed over a period of time. So it incentivizes people to stay and work hard, because the rewards are going to come whenever they decide to leave, as long as they keep the shareholder value high. Now, if they don't work hard, the opposite can happen, the value can go down and they could get nothing.

My philosophy about giving is not necessarily shared by many of my peers but I've always been true to myself and what I whole-heartedly believe is right. I would not sell the company, risking the decimation of the organization and the folks who helped build it. Closing the doors was a fleeting thought which lasted about 2.35 seconds.

Perhaps, like me, you have invested most of your time, energy and life into building your legacy? Or perhaps you are on the verge of building one now? At whichever stop along your path to achievement you find yourself at this moment, having an effective Exit Strategy which lines up with your values, principles and retirement plans is crucial to your overall fulfillment.

Where am I? What do I want now? What am I willing to do? What am I willing to give up? What is it going to take? These are crucial, difficult questions you must ask yourself if you are considering going the ESOP route.

Extensive preparation before, diligent pursuit during, and acute awareness of the aftermath of creating an ESOP is what Exit Strategy provides. Beyond the neatly presented power points and well-suited financial professionals, the business owner must be positioned to crunch numbers, gather documents, choose and train successors, all while running the business, and working to convert the attitudes and beliefs of the people who were comfortable as employees. Successfully converting an organization to an ESOP also means looking in the mirror and taking a new position. The entrepreneurial spirit is not one which naturally resonates throughout the vibrational pull of those 9-to-6ers which have become comfortable with receiving a weekly paycheck along with weekends off, cushy benefits and unlimited copies, pens and sticky notes.

Get prepared for twists, turns, fast starts and slow going when considering your own Exit Strategy. Fore to the future...

Reward Requires Effort

"Most entrepreneurs live the way most people won't, so they can live the way most people can't."
– Tony Thompson

If employees work hard, everyone wins. If they don't work hard, the company's value goes down. They continue get a check every two weeks and when they retire, they don't get anything. All of the sacrifices made in the beginning are long forgotten by most. A lot of people see where we are today, but they don't remember what it took to get here. I wanted employees to share in the rewards of the company, but there's always a downside. Most people want to look at the upside and they don't ever want to look at the downside.

The Transaction And The Transition

———🕴———

To be successful in business you have to be able to see the future. Without personal vision and passion, attitudes become barriers within the ESOP transition.

Ownership Requires Acceptance

The ESOP provides ownership and incentivizes people to stay and to work hard because they can receive a bigger reward. In our case, shared ownership – the profits from the company – I gave up future profits to pay off the debt. It's like having a 401k but employees don't necessarily have to wait until they retire. As the company owner, with the support of professional advisors, you get to make the decision about the length of time you allocate for vesting. In my case, we structured 100% allocation over 12 years. The Trust we structured allots stock shares based on salary and vests at six years. After six years in the ESOP structure, employees can leave with ½ of what their total allocation will be. If employees reach 12 years, while they are fully vested, they can take their full retirement at the age of 65.

There are too many people who go to school, get a degree and end up getting a job in an area they didn't go to school for. Some start businesses the same way. I've been blessed to be able to do what I went to school for and what I was trained to do. That's why it frustrates me sometimes when everybody does not have the same passion that I have, even now that we're an ESOP.

I often thought about how I would transition, knowing once I sell the company, all bets are off, I couldn't protect the employees. I could have sold the company to the firm who offered to buy it. I would have made a nice amount of profit, and they would have made money, and then fired all the people.

I decided against it because I didn't build my company for it to simply dissolve and leave my loyal employees unemployed and perhaps destitute. My vision included all of us having ease in retirement, not just me and my immediate family. However, the problem, perhaps not as unique to my company as one might believe, was that they hadn't really amassed wealth in the retirement programs offered throughout the years. Collectively, they wouldn't have much to show for the years they put in if the company was sold, unprotected by me.

Getting to the transaction was a transition. It took quite a bit of research, investment and preparation. Beyond the semantics and systems, there are still the people. Position makes a difference. It changes the posture. Posture includes attitudes, habits, behaviors and ease of being "employed," in this case, which created a ground-swell of challenges and changes.

A group of people who regularly didn't contribute to their retirements were not going to overnight say, "I'm excited about being an owner in this new company structure, now let's start saving, cutting needless expenses and behave as if our salaries depend on it!"

It's not as simple as putting the ESOP in place and all of a sudden everybody's is going to get it. They don't. Everybody is not born to be entrepreneurs, nor do they want to be entrepreneurs. There are a lot of people who want to be told what to do. That's something that a lot of people don't like to admit. When you analyze people, there are some who don't want to be the person in charge. They don't want to have that responsibility. They don't want to be the guy responsible for someone else. You know the stance, "Tell me what you want me to do; I'm going to do it, and pay me when I get done." That's what most of the workforce is.

As you are preparing for your conversion, consider the people and the process.

Is An ESOP Right For You?

Where do you see the ownership of your company in the next 5 to 10 years? What do you want your legacy to be? Which available exit strategies will meet these expectations?

You can sell the company externally.

You can sell the entire company internally.

You can sell a portion of the company internally…

You can even sell your company internally in such a way that neither you nor the employees have to pay for the company shares up front – the profits from the company can pay for it.

These are all good reasons to choose the ESOP Exit Strategy.

ESOP
BASICS

———🕴———

Defining the ESOP

An Employee Stock Ownership Plan ("ESOP") is a "qualified employee retirement plan" designed to invest primarily in stock of the sponsoring company.

A unique combination of a leveraged buyout and an employee benefit plan, the ESOP can be used in basic or very complex transactions. An ESOP can be an effective way of facilitating fractional or total ownership transition and allows the owners to sell parts of the company over time.

Tax Incentives and Benefits

Congress has created tax incentives which most business owners find quite interesting.

- Tax deductibility of the entire payment to service transaction debt benefits the company.

- Tax benefits to the employees include a non-contributory, tax-deferred retirement account.

- Tax benefits to the selling shareholders include deferral of capital gain on sale to the ESOP Trust if you meet certain requirements.

ESOP Trustee

ESOPs require the appointment of an ESOP Trustee as an advocate for the participants. The trustee must review and approve the transaction. Trustees must use their own independent financial and legal advisors.

The ESOP Provides Flexibility

A great advantage of the ESOP is creating a structure which suits your company's unique makeup. When I started talking ESOP originally, I was going to sell 100% of the company, making employees 100% owners. Then I switched to 51/49%. This would be beneficial for several reasons.

First, I wasn't ready to walk away. If I sold it to them, entirely, I would have lost total control and would have been out. Second, I knew there was still work to be done as far as getting everyone's mindset around ownership. Their mindsets directly affect performance and productivity in a new, more direct way as owners and we all needed some adjustments. Third, I could continue to be an influential leader within the organization. Fourth, I make myself available to bridge those relationships

I have developed with people in the industry to my successor.

Flexibility can benefit everyone and the organization. You can choose to sell 100% of your company to the employees or a portion. Even at 100%, they don't take over ownership right away. It's not immediate. The ESOP is a mechanism of creating and transferring ownership, over a period of time, which you can customize. That's another distinction to selling it right out. An ESOP allows you time to allocate shares to the employees over an established time period. You determine what that period of time should be. When considering how long the allocation period should be, I created a roster to help lay out the facts. I looked at their ages, positions, and skill levels. Then, coupled with the note (the debt period), I made a choice. I didn't want all the debt to be paid off and everyone get their shares allocated at the same time, because they could potentially leave.

I staggered the debt payoff period and the allocation shares. Based on the average age of my employees, I tried to calculate the time periods in a way which was beneficial to the company and the younger employees. I was concerned not only with the vesting period but also the age at which most would become eligible for retirement. Because if not, those who didn't leave when they became vested would be eligible to leave once they become eligible for retirement. If that were to happen, it would have a negative impact on the value of the remaining shares available for the younger employees.

Be realistic about where you are and where you are headed. Don't forget the external factors which will influence your choices – including competition.

RELATIONSHIPS AND MOTIVES

In many instances the successful owner doesn't care much about the individual employees or their interests, and they don't associate with their employees. That's a problem. If you are serious about using the ESOP as an *Exit Strategy*, you've got to have good relationships with your people and they must trust your motives. You have to be educated about the details of everything in order for you to articulate to the employees and educate them on the process. Once they understood how ESOP(s) worked, they started feeling a little more comfortable. I learned this during our transition.

When I first talked about the ESOP, people were skeptical. Thinking this is just a money thing for me, until I started explaining certain aspects of it. My stance:

First of all, I don't have to do this. Second, it's not costing you anything for me to do this, but I'm giving up half of what I built to do it. Third, all you have to do is continue to do what you're doing and you're going to walk away with, potentially, on the average, a quarter of a million dollars that you wouldn't have had before.

That still sounds too good to be true to most people, because thieves look for theft. And then that just goes back to the character of the individual, you can't do anything about that, because most people, given the situation, wouldn't make the same choice.

Second, at the point that the ESOP loan is paid off by the company, assuming if we perform at the current level, the company would then have over $100k per month freed up to go toward the bottom line, which is the net income/ profit.

Third, work hard now, be cost conscious, and walk away with a nest egg when you are vested. It's like getting free money because you continue to earn your salaries while helping to bring in business, sustain existing clients and continue to deliver stellar service. As long as we do that, everyone who stays with the company for 6 years, the vesting period, and certainly 12 years will have a windfall.

Our close relationships and the fact that we were a big business in small body were factors in our favor. Also, we began preparing for the transaction when the company was about 18 years old. Many of the employees had been there for over a decade, and some of them were related to me. We built the business together through weddings, births, deaths, anniversaries, celebrations, and loyalty.

The Details Can Be Cumbersome

When considering employees, timelines and percentages of ownership, the details can be cumbersome during your ESOP transitional experience, especially if you're a small business.

I'm still on the hook for a lot of things. My name is still on the line of credit. If your business has qualified as a SBE, WBE, MBE, DBE, VOSB or other, keeping up with those certifications takes effort. I provide the information needed. The paperwork itself would have been cumbersome to have now all the owners, each owner, to have to share all that financial data on each individual every time, every year, that we're trying to get certification. By maintaining 51% ownership, only I still have to do that. So it's a certain amount of inconvenience and invasion of privacy that I have to put up with and that I have to go through, but I felt like it was easier and better for me to do it, just one person, as opposed to all these people. Plus, you never know in the next 12 years of full conversion, how many of the employees are going to come and go. It would be a change every time somebody left.

You'll need to continue to check your motives along the way. Remembering that just because you care, it doesn't mean others will. You have to also help them to understand why any of this is important.

The reality? Some people don't care what happens to the company 20 years from now. Some will remain, some will go, and many aren't even thinking about retirement or doing things differently. The ones who are vested – and have invested – may think once they are eligible for the full payoff, they are done, and not concerned with what happens to others or the structure/company. Just remember that, especially if the company has been your passion.

What's Important To You?

If you've owned your company for at least ten years, you care. So when you're making these decisions you need to think about what you care about. For some, it is going to be "I want to make sure the employees are well off," or "I want to make sure my dream doesn't die."

For others it may be their legacy and that's how they're planning to fund their foundations or hobbies. Some people know they're not ready to retire, but they want to be able to have this space to groom and make some good business decisions.

Which are you?

COMPANY VALUE

———🏃———

Educate yourself about the true market value of your company.

Likely, you have a *business plan*, even if it's the dusty one from 24 years ago, which you've loosely followed. Regardless of when it was created, you need one today to remind you of your vision and intent. Charting where you were and where you want to go will also support you in creating a strategically focused *succession plan*. To pull off a successful *Exit Strategy*, to make the transition, beyond transaction, you're going to need an open mind, willingness to learn and to listen. As a business owner you may not want to hear what I'm going to say, but you need to hear it because nobody in your own organization will say it to your face.

In order to be in position to sell your company or to make your company attractive enough to be sold, you have to know what that entails. Sometimes you can think your company is worth more than it is. You can believe your own press, your own hype, or your own whatever. But what I quickly learned is that it doesn't matter what I think. It's all about what the market says the company's worth. And if the company is based on the founder being at the helm, if something happens to the founder then it's not worth anything.

Just because you've been in business for fifteen, twenty years, doesn't mean you know it all. Because you've been so busy honing your skills, crafting your trade of that business, you did not learn all the details. And I think that's a big mistake that people make, skimming over the particulars of what your company has morphed into.

When you don't understand the details of every aspect of your business, it's hard for you to put together a strategy, objectively. It's hard for you to even put a value on it because you don't know what it takes to make this whole, big machine run.

FORESIGHT AND PLANNING

The most revenue doesn't always equate to the most profit. Re-engineering the company growth and relevance means being savvy about Product Life Cycles.

Product Life Cycle

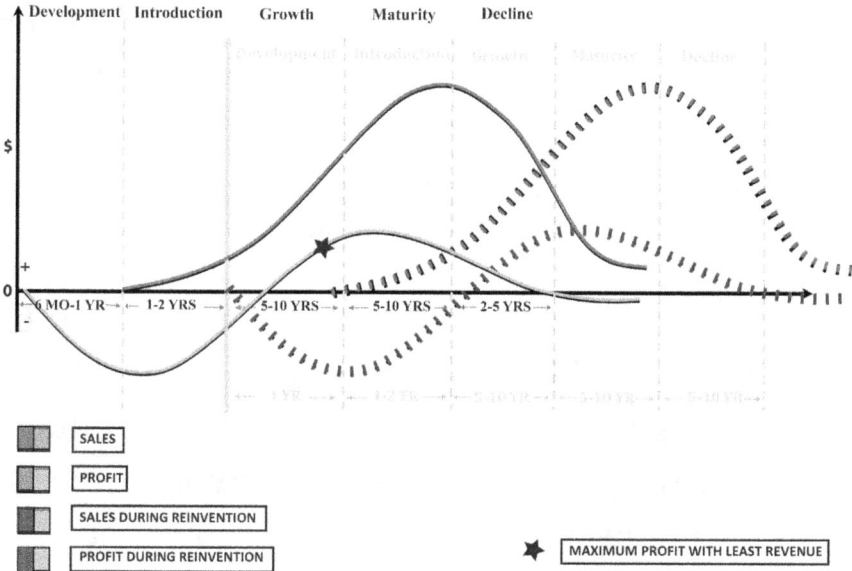

Development | Introduction | Growth | Maturity | Decline

$

+

0

-

←6 MO-1 YR→ ←— 1-2 YRS —→ ←5-10 YRS→ ←— 5-10 YRS —→ ←— 2-5 YRS—→

SALES

PROFIT

SALES DURING REINVENTION

PROFIT DURING REINVENTION

★ MAXIMUM PROFIT WITH LEAST REVENUE

In my experience, the basic phases of any product or service are the same regardless of the particular product or service. When you have a service company like ours, you reach a maturity point where the product gets stale and you start to decline in revenue and profit. Factors could be the economy, competition, aging workforce, or technology, for example. Therefore, you must reinvent the company to maintain relevance in the market. This chart reflects, in my experience, the best time to implement that change. It's typically during the growth phase of your product or service.

There's a point on the curve where you can maximize your profit with the least amount of effort. Surprisingly enough, it's not the point where you generate the most revenue. Notice the star. It's the point where you are generating the most profit with the least effort. This is a good thing. There is a point in every company where this is true.

Every business school teaches the product life cycle. I simply shifted this chart over, with the dotted lines representing the time to introduce a new (product) cycle. When you have the most cash at your disposal is the opportune reinvention/introduction phase.

While you are making money you want to create a new cycle (product or service) at the same you are generating the most revenue and the most profit with a previously introduced product or service. Doing so will allow you to grow while reaching the maturity stage in the product or service previously introduced.

When you have a level or average profit over a sustainable growth a profit over a period of time, you are able to stay in business and succeed. Ideally, you want the overall trend to go up. Yet there are times when it may be level and you don't want your company to start losing money, so it's important to be aware and make decisions accordingly, for your organization.

VALUATION

———👔———

These factors will determine whether your company is a good fit for an ESOP. Having an understanding of what drives value is critical to the decision to sell and when to sell. Value reflects the current characteristics of your company.

EXTERNAL DRIVERS
Market Multiples
Lending Conditions
Interest Rates
Industry Trends
Investor Psychology
Capital Markets - Debt/Equity
Economic Policies
Political Environment
International Markets
Competition

INTERNAL DRIVERS

Growth Prospects
Profitability
Revenue Sources
Balance Sheet
Intangible Assets
Management Team
Customer Diversification
Size
Capital Requirements
Litigation & Environmental

After reviewing these items, be sure your value expectations are realistic.

Feasibility

———👤———

Now that value is established, a feasibility analysis is the next step.

It is important to consider how the ESOP transaction impacts your company's debt borrowing capacity and future cash flows, in addition to how it changes ongoing employee benefit levels.

In order to perform an in-depth ESOP feasibility study, internal and external attributes must be considered.

INTERNAL ATTRIBUTES
Ownership Mix
Cash Flow
Balance Sheet
Capital Structure
Historical Performance

Facilities and Equipment
Management
Employee Benefit Levels

EXTERNAL ATTRIBUTES
Market Factors
Industry Dynamics
Equity and Debt Capital Markets
Competition
Suppliers
ESOP Financing

Access to this information should be readily available for your use. If you have a hard time answering these questions, you have a lot of internal homework to do.

Transitioning Senior Management

———🧑‍💼———

Employees are one of your biggest assets. Part of the value of hiring younger people, or recent college grads, is that they may be more familiar with what the market will bear now, and what's going on with the market, whereas you may be out of touch.

You're out dated. Yeah, you're out of touch. Because it goes to that chart, when I talk about reinventing the company, but you also have to reinvent yourself. If you're not constantly updating yourself on what's going on in the trends, in the industry, in the world and everything else, your value goes down. You become a dinosaur. And you have to bring in new blood. You have to have a balance of senior people and young people in your organization. You want the senior people to transfer the knowledge they've gained through the years to the younger people, that knowledge and experience it would take them years to get. And you want the younger people to use their creativity and their innovative savvy in technology to take it to the next level. You have to be able to let go and allow the creativity of others to continue to move your vision forward, because your vision is going to change, as you are transitioning out.

One of your biggest challenges will be to grow the mindsets of the managers and employees because they never had to be "responsible" for the company before. Their employment was not dependent on how much we saved at the copier in the past. However, in shared ownership, they need to know how much the color prints cost, and perhaps they won't waste as much and will make sure others don't either. Efficiency, curtailing costs and reducing spending have not been priorities to them. Most don't have financial literacy and now they've inherited the business without knowing anything about business.

How far will you go? Ask yourself, "Do I try to educate them on business or do I just try to help them understand why they shouldn't be wasteful?"

I suggest doing a quick calculation of what "Coming in late and leaving early," is costing the company on a monthly basis. They will likely be shocked and hopefully more responsible, across the board.

NAMING A SUCCESSOR

———— 👤 ————

"They can't take your place but they can fill your space."

The person I chose to succeed me as president, of all my technical people, has probably been there the shortest amount of time. The other guys, who've been with me the longest, are engineers who are technically competent, but most engineers are not people persons. They don't necessarily have the personalities nor are they extroverted. They don't like selling and their strengths aren't in marketing or networking, per se. To succeed me in the role of president, you've got to do all of that and more.

If you're going to be the leader of the organization you've got to motivate people. You've got to sell. You must continuously sell and market the company. Most technical people are not salespeople. They want to work on projects. They get the job done and you need people to get the job done. As a leader you have to be able to assess your people and know their individual strengths and weaknesses. Once you identify who you have, you must make decisions, not based on who you like and how long they've been there, or based on "He's my buddy," or "She's my relative." You can't do that if you want the company to survive.

I've always looked at the Vice President of Business Development role as a critical component to the organization because that's the person who has to understand what we do, how we do it, and be able to go out and market and sell it. The person I chose to replace me was in this position and was the logical choice. He was an electrical engineer so he was skilled in the craft, the primary aspect of the business, and he had the business acumen. He had been working with the company for about seven years prior to being named as my successor. I had already identified him as a leader. When I first started putting the ESOP together, I didn't know at that time. As the process continued, it became clearer.

Creating a list of expectations will assist you as you turn over the reigns. This list should be mutual – from you and from your successor. It will assist everyone in the communication process and also in misunderstandings, potential conflicts and leadership challenges. It will help in perception and in reality. If you learn, early, to work well in your new role, you will ultimately empower your successor and build confident leaders who are able to solve problems and grow the operation without you.

Five Necessary Steps For Internal Team Success

———— 👤 ————

So you've been doing the same thing for a long time and you've got a certain amount of success now, but now you're going to have to start thinking about how you're going to get out of it. It's going to take your thinking to change. It's going to take your doing to change. It's going to take your willingness to step out of the way and getting rid of the bottlenecks. Because sometimes you can be the bottleneck, you have to ask yourself are you coachable, are you teachable?

#1. Document Your Experiences So They Can Be Duplicated

Your ideas, experiences, habits, quick fixes, and work ethic, all the factors which got you to this point of being successful, whatever they are, you need to document. Clearly identify steps to implement the ones which should be carried on, and which ones may be foundations for innovation. Documentation is important because there are things specific to you, which you did, that got you here. Many of those activities can be duplicated if you sit down and think long and hard about what those qualities and things were.

Start with a list of at least 7 mistakes you've made, why you made them, what you learned through them, and why you consider them important enough to share. As you focus on the small things you did to grow the business, it'll be easier to share *solutions* and record them too. They will serve as invaluable wisdom and knowledge for the present and for the future.

#2. Evaluate Your Current Employees Carefully

Get your employee roster and get to work with these questions to ask yourself:

a.   Who are my managers?

b.   Who are my potential managers?

c.   What are their capabilities?

d. What are their ages?

e. How technically competent are they?

f. How good are their soft-skills?

g. Who's likely to want more responsibility?

h. Which persons are comfortable and complacent?

i. Who seems to be hungry and passionate?

j. Who's already working hard?

k. Who's the dead weight?

l. How am I really defining leadership and who's already displaying it?

m. Who can bring in new business?

n. Who's ready to be downsized or retired?

o. What don't I know?

p. Who don't I know?

q. Who's reliable, dependable, respected and confident?

r. Who are they likely to listen to besides me?

s. How much do I really want to share ownership?

t. Who are my personal favorites and why?

u. Who are the team players?

v. Who are the time wasters, moral busters and space takers?

w. How long will it take for (them) to be groomed and ready to lead?

x. Who can assist me objectively and honestly during the ESOP transition?

y. Is my team interested in becoming an ESOP?

z. What have I missed?

After you answer these questions, you'll need to evaluate and acknowledge the next steps. Tough choices must follow.

Identify people in various positions throughout the organization who are the performance leaders. Department heads should document what they do and how they do it well. Don't rely on memory because people need detailed documentation so it can be duplicated. You never know when someone will chose to leave, and certainly some will, especially when the transition is becoming a reality.

People are going to use their own ingenuity, style, preferences and experience to get things done. Your experience and influence can assist them with perspective and efficiency. You want to allow them a certain level of flexibility to carry your vision to create new norms.

#3. Groom Successors Intentionally

Once you've identified that person or persons you have to personally spend time with them to ensure that they can do it the job. Do the job not necessarily the way you would do it, but do it none-the-less. You must personally spend time to ensure the company will carry on and expand. Mutual respect, solid relationships and exceptional communication are invaluable here.

#4. Back Off Appropriately

I suggest you step back if you are still too passionate to walk away completely. Insuring the company continues to grow must be bigger than title, position, ego or pay check. The transition from "source to resource" is an ongoing opportunity which will increase your endurance, improve performance and test your patience. This is the hardest step. The company must grow, which means you have to let go. You have back off and allow them to make mistakes, which is one of the hardest parts, because they're going to make mistakes and it's going to be painful. It's going to be painful to watch. But it's almost like you have to in order for them to get it. Your reference notes and recommendations will assist them and you to make it through the process.

#5. Go From Founder to Chief Dream Officer

Hold on to the big picture and give the reigns to your successor to execute instead of occupying both places. Once your operational person (company president, in my case) is in place then you make yourself available as a resource to these people as they carry on your mission. Don't interfere, but make yourself available and let them know that they're not by themselves. They can get into their new roles and start doing stuff, yet thinking they can't. When they think, "How do I do this?" They need to remember, all they've got to do is call you. This is bigger than the call. It's also about humility and overcoming any pride or power struggle issues. As the visionary, it's up to you to provide the tools and the open lines of communication. You've got to keep yourself available.

Cultivating relationships within the organization may not have been a high priority in the past. If that's the case, you have work to do. You're going to need your soft-skills to ease the transition into an effectively transitioning ESOP.

Experience and people are your most valuable assets.

Team Of Experts

———👤———

You need a team of experts to complete the ESOP transaction. Some of these experts will be people you will use on an ongoing basis, and others will be one time service providers. Services you'll need to include are Annual Evaluations, Periodic Audits, as well as on-going Legal and Financial Services.

The Company, the selling shareholder(s) and the ESOP Trustee all have separate advisors.

The Company needs an attorney, and accountant. The Company also needs a financial advisor who provides the annual valuations to the Trustee on their behalf, and the financial institution that is providing the financing for the buyout.

The selling owner needs a separate attorney, accountant and financial institution that is financing the transaction. The financial advisor provides the one-time valuation for the seller.

The Trustee is representing the company shareholders, serving as the middleman between the seller and the new shareholders. They will allocate the shares of the company to the new shareholders once the sale is complete. The trustee needs a financial advisor to provide annual valuations for the new shareholders.

Loyalty, trust and a professional working relationship is essential throughout the transaction. Keep in mind, your selection of this team is crucial to allow for a smooth transaction, as it is a process.

CLOSING

Closing the transaction requires the seller and the ESOP Trustee to negotiate terms of the final deal.

Steps to closing include:

- Negotiation of Terms

- Final Term Sheet

- Transaction Documents
  - SPA (Stock Purchase Agreement)
  - Fairness Opinion
  - Various Other Legal Documents
  - Bank Agreements

Be prepared, for the long closing meeting. I had a conference room table full of multiple copies of stacks of documents which took about two hours to review and sign. Depending on how your company is structured will determine the magnitude of the people and documents which will be needed to close.

THE AFTERMATH

———⚡———

Communicating how the ESOP works should be your focus. Sharing what did and will happen as the new entity takes patience, good communication skills and a thorough understanding of how all of this is to operate. You must take your time and be careful as you answer questions and set new expectations. Details matter. The impact of how well you share information, in a way which matters to the new employee owners is absolutely vital to the transition because the ESOPs performance is tied to company performance. Therefore it is imperative that the employee owners understand that impact.

Research shows that ESOP companies that communicate and share meaningful information outperform those who do not.

Don't expect improved performance unless the participants get the connection between what they do every day, how that impacts earnings and how earnings impact the Company's value.

WORKING BOOK

———— 💼 ————

Personal Reflection, Professional Success Questions and Lecture Notes

The following pages are your opportunity to download your brain. Perhaps you've been too busy or consumed to focus on what got you to this point in your career? Before you move on to something else, think and document. Working through this section will support you and those who need to trust your leadership, without you.

It's time to get going!
Tony

1

CURRENT CONDITION
NEEDING RESOLUTION

———👤———

Who's involved? What's at stake? If it's not resolved what's the worst that could happen? Who would be affected? What's the primary reason this is happening? What am I willing to do about it? Why does it matter?

Who needs to do what by when?

....

....

....

....

....

....

....

....

....

....

....

....

....

....

....

....

....

....

....

....

....

....

....

....

....

....

....

....

....

....

....

....

....

....

....

....

....

2
BIG IDEAS FOR THE FUTURE

———👔———

I've thought about this over the years but didn't act upon it. If I flesh it out, it could be of benefit to...

BIG IDEA #1

....

....

....

....

....

....

....

....

BIG IDEA #2

....

....

....

....

....

....

....

....

....

....

....

....

....

....

3

LIFE EXPERIENCES

———👤———

My life and career have taught me some big lessons. I realize they shaped my thoughts, actions, behaviors and the way I've run the company. These are 3 meaningful things which could be valuable when I share them.

LIFE EXPERIENCE # 1

....

....

....

....

....

....

....

....

LIFE EXPERIENCE #2

....

....

....

....

....

....

....

....

....

....

....

....

....

....

....

LIFE EXPERIENCE # 3

....

....

....

....

....

....

....

....

....

....

....

....

....

....

4
Quick Fixes

———— 👔 ————

With change comes challenges and choices. When the pressure has mounted these are 4 ways I've relieved it throughout the years.

Quick Fix #1

....

....

....

....

....

....

....

....

QUICK FIX #2

....

....

....

....

....

....

....

....

QUICK FIX #3

....

....

....

....

....

....

....

QUICK FIX #4

....

....

....

....

....

....

....

....

....

....

....

....

....

....

5

REGRETS

With experience, I acknowledge there are some things I could have thought or done differently. Though I can't change what happened before, I write them here so they can be released, revisited or considered today. Being busy, productive and in charge cost me a lot, after all.

REGRET # 1

....

....

....

....

....

....

REGRET # 2

....

....

....

....

....

....

....

....

REGRET # 3

....

....

....

....

....

....

....

REGRET # 4

....

....

....

....

....

....

....

REGRET # 5

....

....

....

....

....

....

....

6

HABITS

These habits brought me here. I may or may not recommend them to others. By documenting them, it will help others and maybe even me.

HABIT # 1

....

....

....

....

....

....

....

....

HABIT # 2

....

....

....

....

....

....

....

....

HABIT # 3

....

....

....

....

....

....

....

HABIT # 4

....

....

....

....

....

....

....

HABIT # 5

....

....

....

....

....

....

....

HABIT # 6

....

....

....

....

....

....

....

....

....

....

....

....

....

....

....

7

MISTAKES

———⊛———

They need to know about these mistakes. If I share them openly, perhaps they will learn from them as well. I will share them accordingly and appropriately, with those who need to know. It feels good to get them out because it's almost time to go.

MISTAKE #1

....

....

....

....

....

....

MISTAKE #2

....

....

....

....

....

....

....

MISTAKE #3

....

....

....

....

....

....

....

MISTAKE #4

....

....

....

....

....

....

....

MISTAKE #5

....

....

....

....

....

....

....

MISTAKE #6

....

....

....

....

....

....

....

....

MISTAKE #7

....

....

....

....

....

....

....

8

Advice Statements

———— 👔 ————

Whether anyone cares or wants to listen, these are my 8 biggest recommendations for my people.

My people at work, at home and in life...

ADVICE STATEMENT #1

....

....

....

....

....

....

....

ADVICE STATEMENT #2

....

....

....

....

....

....

....

....

ADVICE STATEMENT #3

....

....

....

....

....

....

....

ADVICE STATEMENT #4

....

....

....

....

....

....

....

....

ADVICE STATEMENT #5

....

....

....

....

....

....

....

ADVICE STATEMENT #6

....

....

....

....

....

....

....

....

ADVICE STATEMENT #7

....

....

....

....

....

....

....

ADVICE STATEMENT #8

....

....

....

....

....

....

....

....

....

....

....

....

....

....

....

ACKNOWLEDGEMENTS

I'd like to acknowledge the following people for making my journey a smooth and prudent one, as they have displayed the highest level of integrity and professionalism in our dealings:

Tom Reeves for whom without his confidence in my vision, Kwame Building Group may have taken several years to start. He provided the first line of credit and came full circle and provided the ESOP loan.

Pat Buerhing, my current banker, for weathering the tough times and being always available for creative solutions.

My Trust attorney, Ned Riley, for making sure my family was well protected and our future secured. (And for teaching Kristin how to trap shoot).

Mayor Francis Slay for supporting me publicly when it was not so popular for him to do so, and for supporting our organization's efforts while opening doors across the country for which our national presence would not have been possible.

My general counsel and baby brother, Kwame T. Thompson, Esq., for providing me with expert legal counsel and always having my back.

A NOTE FROM THE PUBLISHER

———👤———

Mission Possible Press...

Creating Legacies through Absolute Good Works

As a publisher, I have the opportunity to transform hopeful writers into successful authors. This brings me great pleasure because I believe everyone has wisdom to share and valuable stories to tell.

Dedicated to success, Tony Thompson visualizes what he wants and takes the steps to achieve it. What I have appreciated most about him is his willingness to seek knowledge formally and informally in order to get to his destination. He values scholarship, education and practical life experience to guide him and others to new heights.

Working with Tony to bring his book series to light has been an awesome honor, an adventure, and quite frankly, a rich experience I will always treasure. He shares what he knows, generously. He is dedicated to supporting the success of those willing to work for it. He has unique knowledge coupled with the desire to build a lasting legacy, and has created a functional funnel through which generations shall learn from his example. As iron sharpens iron, get what you can from the wisdom and life of Tony Thompson and soar!

It is my great pleasure to present this book, *Exit Strategy, The ESOP Path to Ultimate Fulfillment*, written by Anthony (Tony) Thompson, as part of our Professional Development Series.

In the Spirit of Communication,

Jo Lena Johnson,
Founder and Publisher
Mission Possible Press
(A division of Absolute Good)
AbsoluteGoodBooks.com

ABOUT THE AUTHOR

———💁———

Anthony (Tony) Thompson is the CEO and Chairman of the Board of Kwame Building Group, Inc. (KWAME), which he founded in 1991. Headquartered in St. Louis, MO, KWAME is a construction management/program management firm that serves as an independent agent to the project owner. KWAME manages projects from conceptualization to construction completion.

An experienced Engineering Professional, Tony held positions with industry leaders prior to building KWAME. Those companies include the Anheuser-Busch Companies, Monsanto Chemical Company and the U.S. Army Corps of Engineers prior to launching KWAME. Never one to rest on his laurels, Tony Thompson believes in education as a means to success. He holds (4) degrees, including a Master of Science in Civil Engineering/Construction Management from Washington University, a Master of Business Administration Degree in Finance from Webster University, and two Bachelor degrees from University of Kansas.

Philanthropically speaking, Tony and his wife Kim have been trail blazers, providing scholarships to college students in the Midwest and throughout the nation, with over $1 million dollars in giving personally, and through the KWAME Foundation. Additionally, Tony has been an active Community Leader and Board Member for some of St. Louis' most respected organizations. They include:

- Founder, KWAME Foundation
- Barnes-Jewish Hospital
- Teach for America
- Regional Business Council
- Boy Scouts of America
- St. Louis Community College Foundation
- Board of Trustees, Webster University
- St. Louis Regional Crime Commission
- St. Louis Black Leadership Roundtable Education

Abbreviated Listing of Special Achievements:

2002	Mayor Francis Slay Business of the Year Award
2002	St. Louis American Salute to Excellence Entrepreneur of the Year Award
2003	Webster University Distinguished Alumni Award
2004	Washington University Distinguished Alumni Award
2004	Saint Louis Council of Construction Consumers MBE of the Year Award
2005 & 2006	Saint Louis Business Journal's Most Influential Leaders
2007	University of Kansas Distinguished Alumni Award
2008	Kappa Alpha Psi Professionalism Award
2011	Salute to Excellence in Education Stellar Performer
2011	Character of Courage Award
2011	FBI Leadership Award
2013	Honorary Doctorate Maryville University
2013	Honorary Doctorate Harris Stowe State University